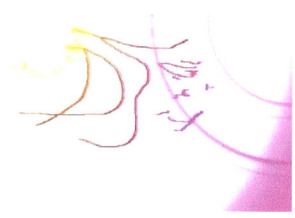

Copyright © 2017 Deborah D Johnson

Published by Aubey, LLC

All rights reserved.

ISBN: 1974024393
ISBN-13: 978-1974024391

DEDICATION

For all those who know that your picture window is the world!

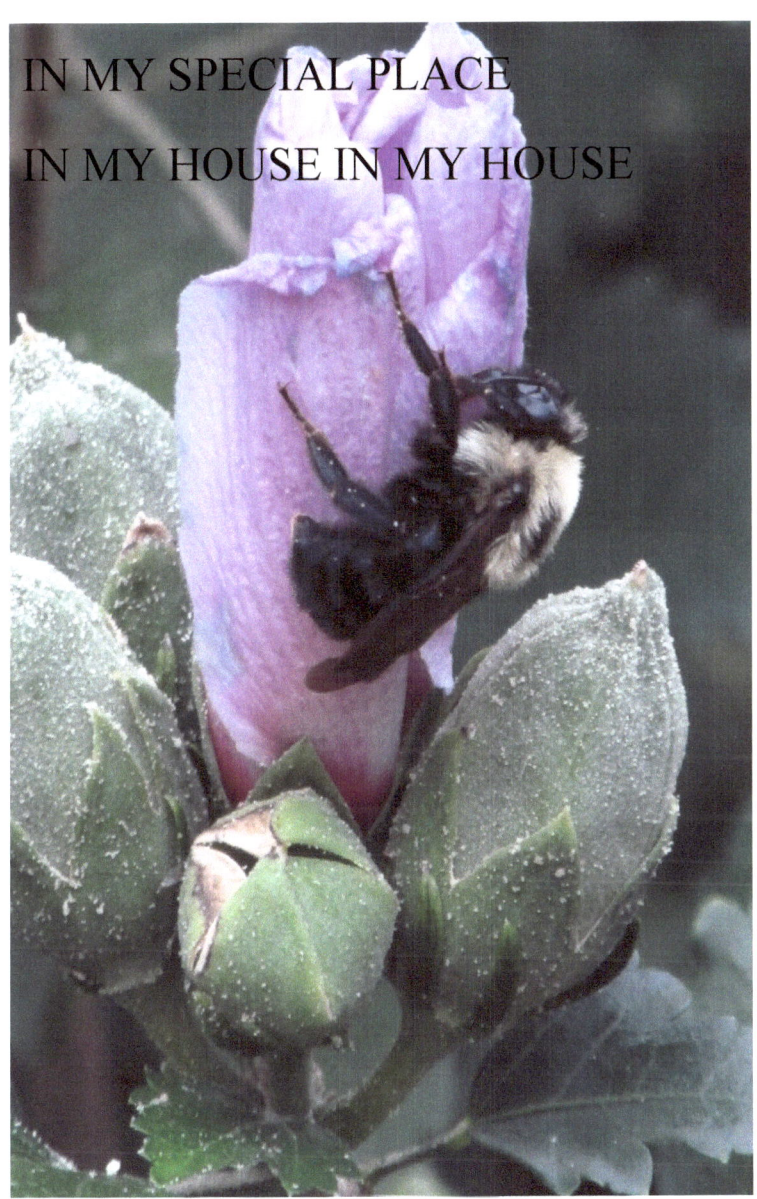

I HAVE A SPECIAL WINDOW

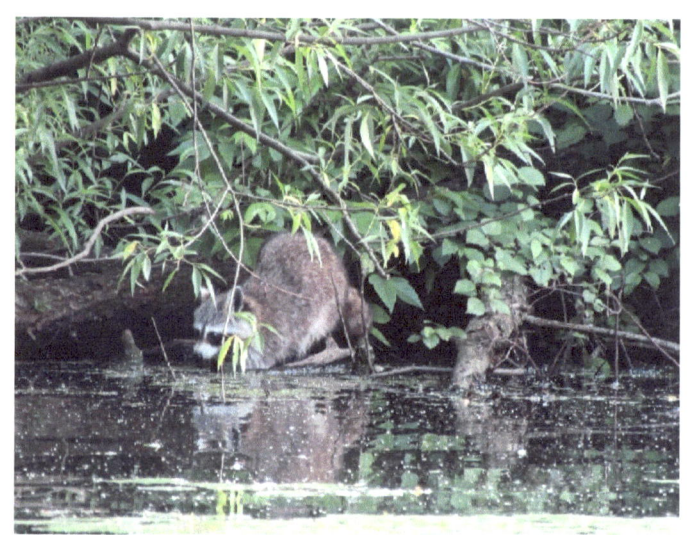

WHERE I'M FREE TO LOOK OUT

I SEE MY SUMMER FLOWERS…

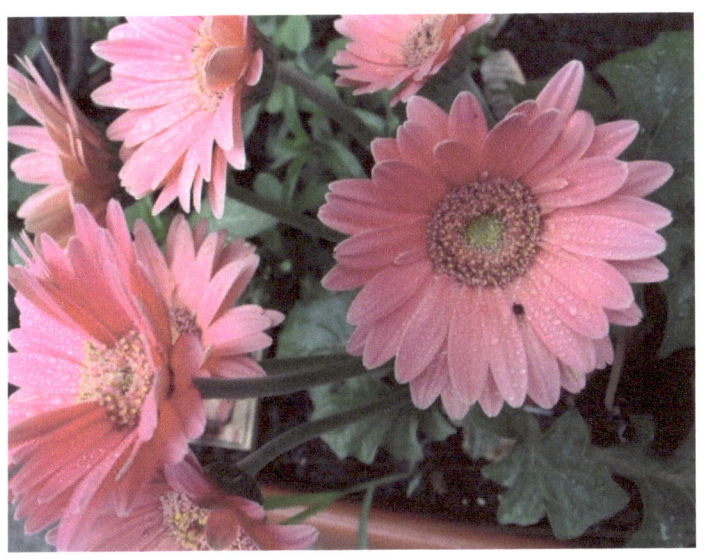

AND THE SUMMER RAIN

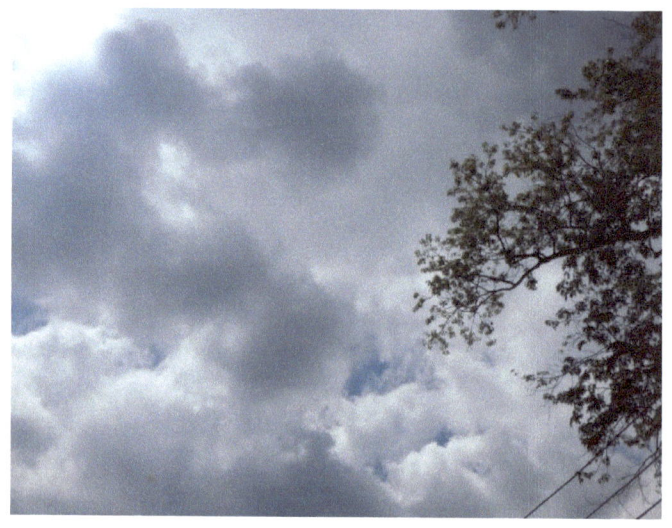

I SEE THE FALL COLORS

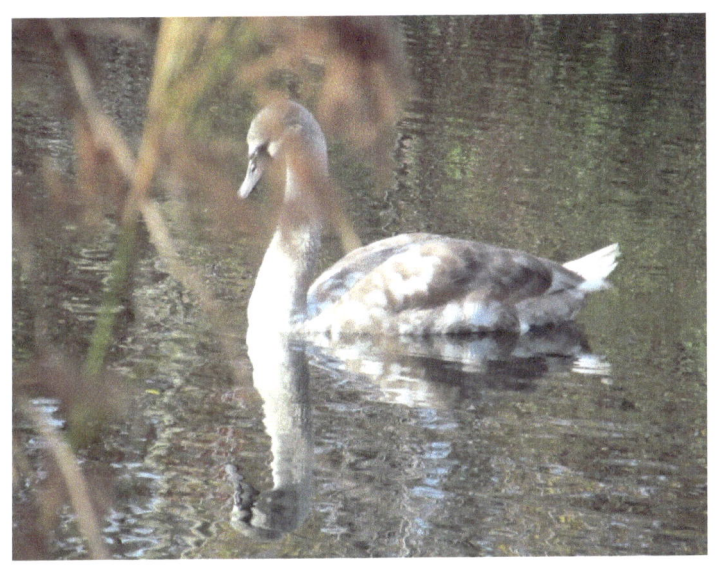

EVEN THE COMING GRAY.

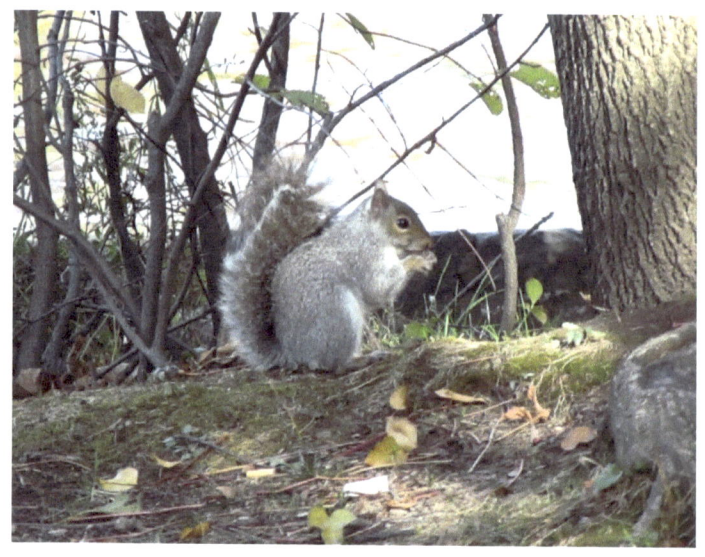

OF THE WINTER WEATHER
FULL OF COLD AND SNOW,

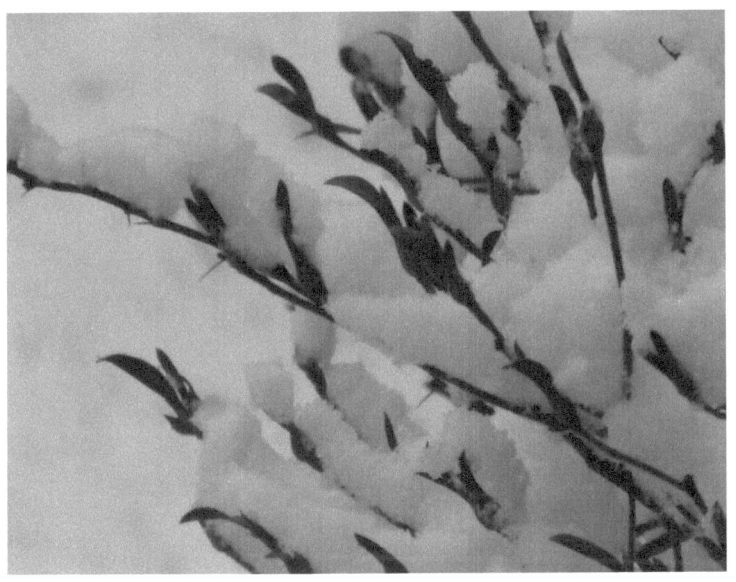

IT LOOKS LOVELY FROM THE INSIDE

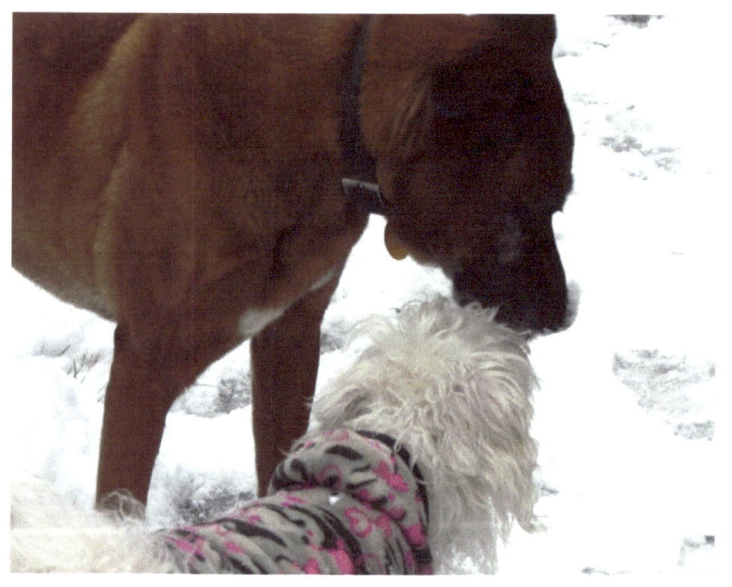

BUT THE OUTSIDE I REFUSE TO GO.

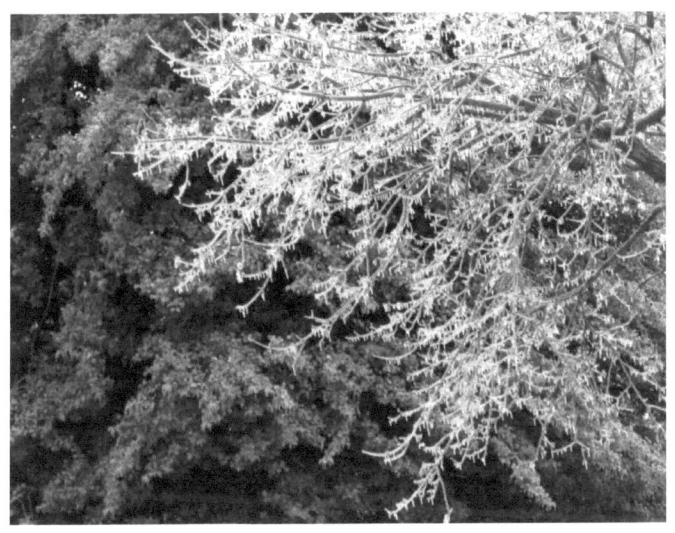

ONE DAY THE VIEW IS
FILLED WITH SNOW.

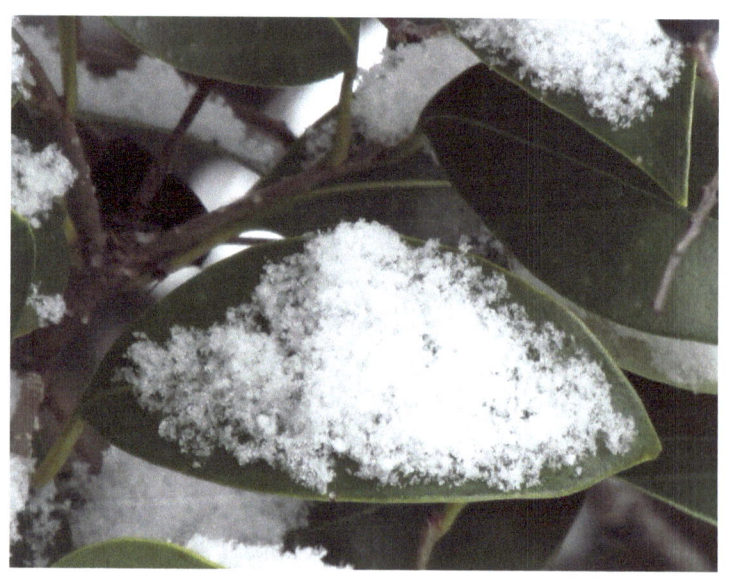

THE NEXT DAY ICEY RAIN.

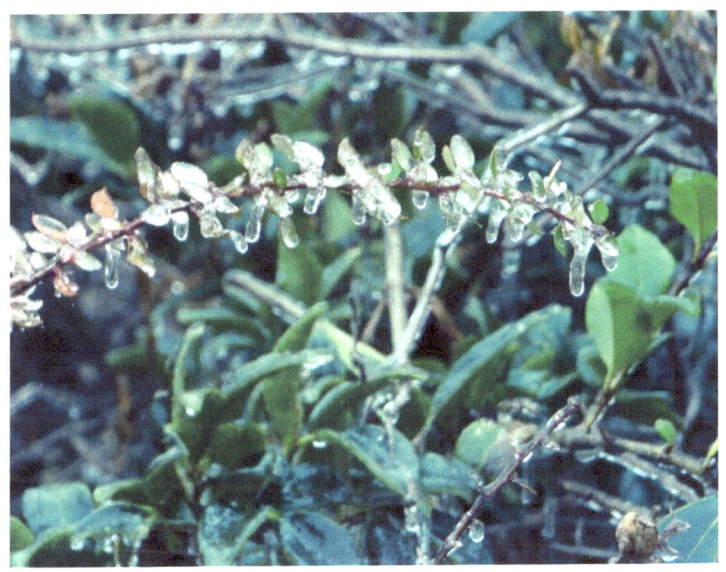

CAN'T WAIT UNTIL THE
SUMMER SUN

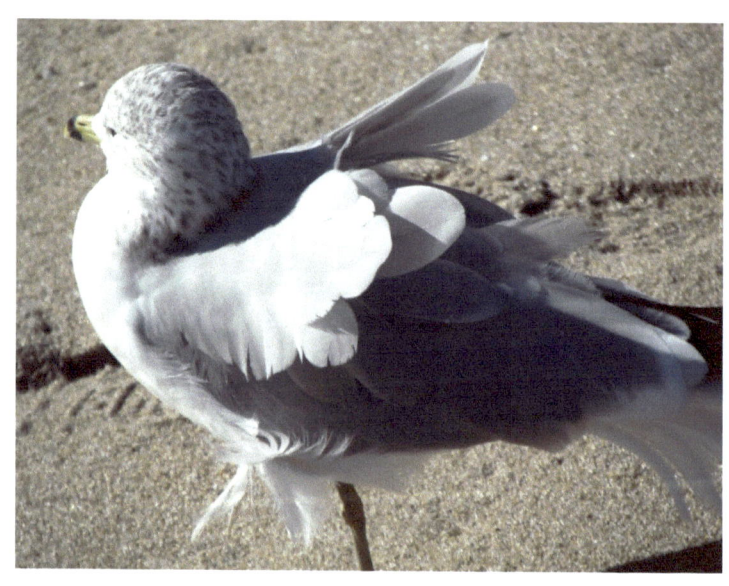

RETURNS TO SHINE AGAIN.

THEN I FINALLY SEE THE COLORS CHANGE

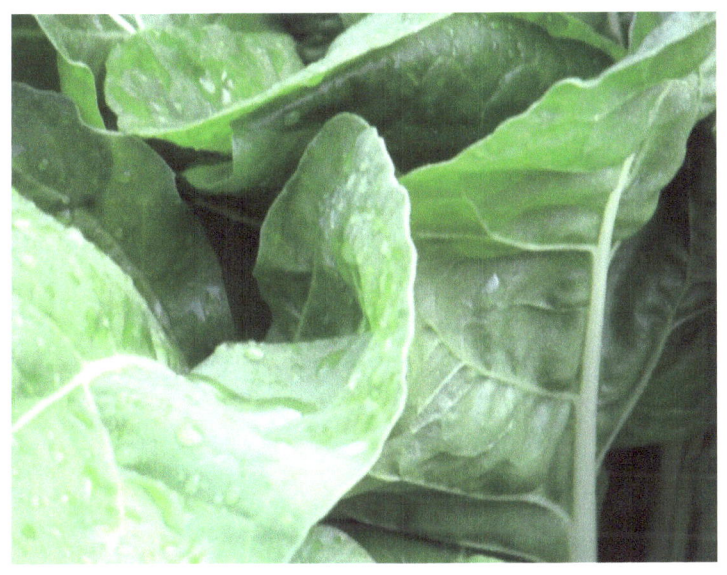

FROM GRAY BACK TO GREEN

AND I SEE THE TREES BLOOMING

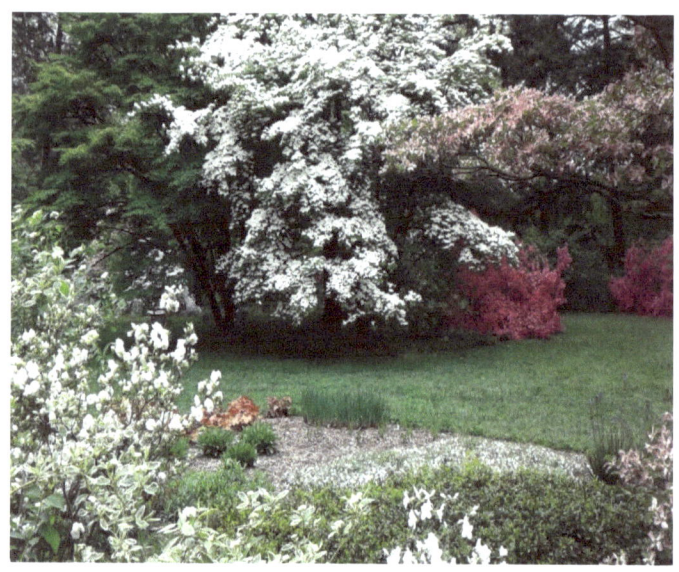

IT'S SUCH A WONDERFUL SCENE.

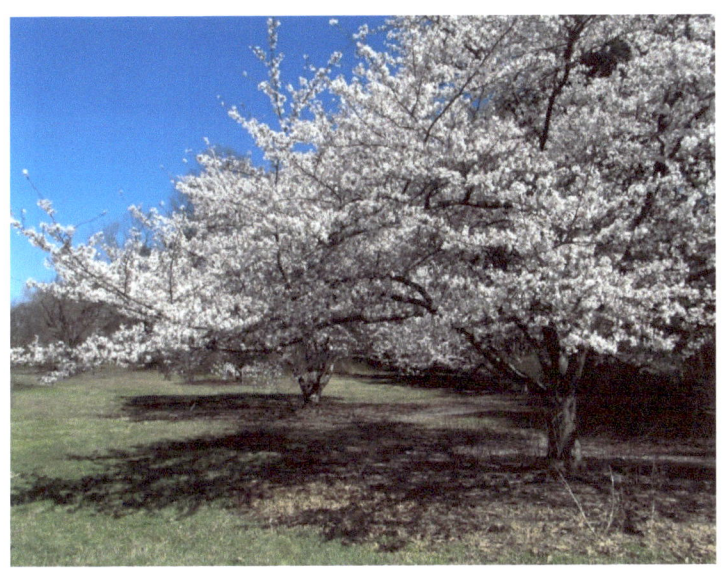

I WANT TO VENTURE OUTSIDE

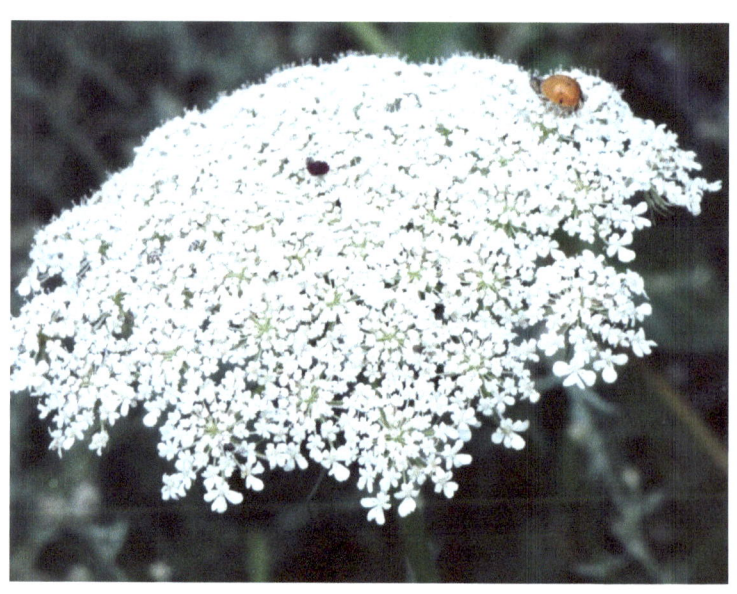

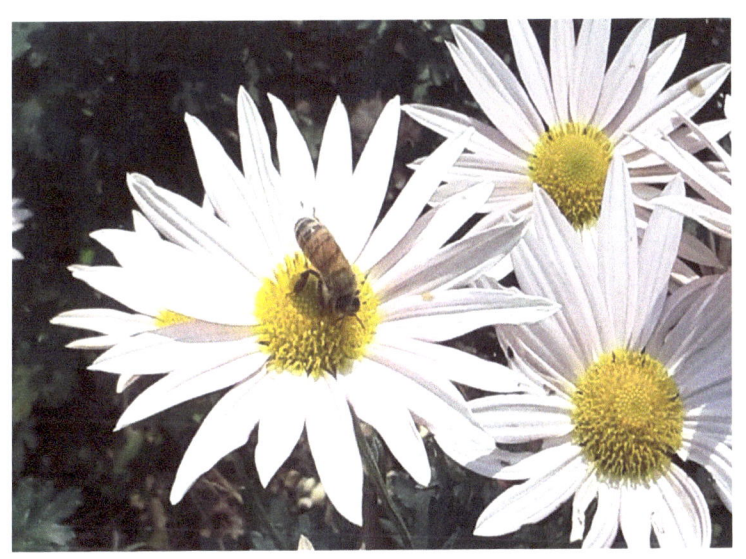

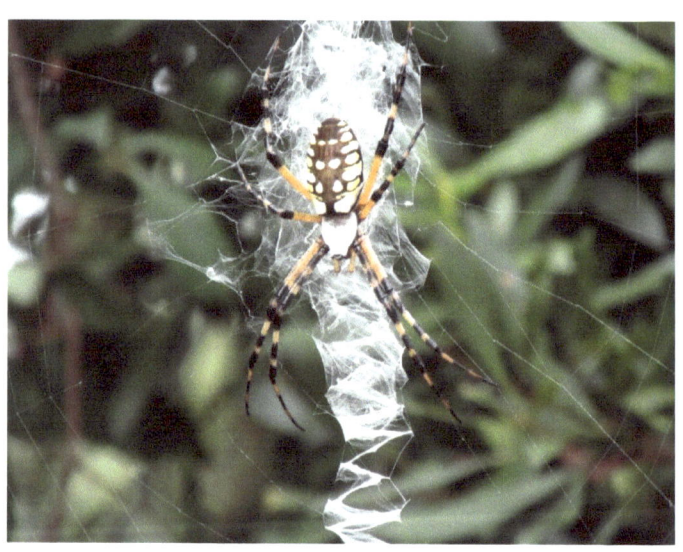

WHEN I SEE THE SUMMER COME

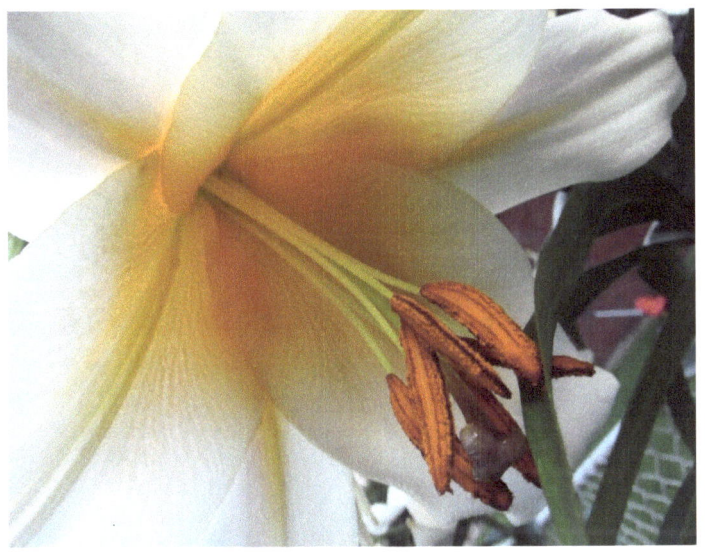

I CAN AGAIN PLANT LOVELY FLOWERS

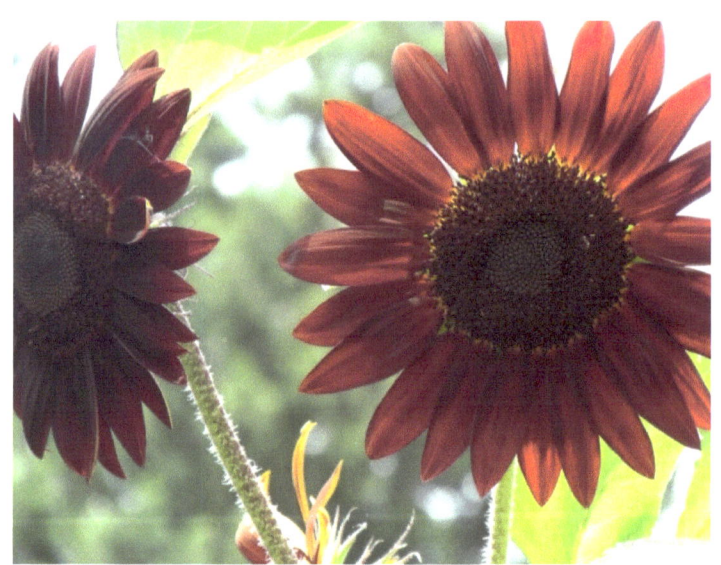

AND ENJOY THE SUMMER SUN.

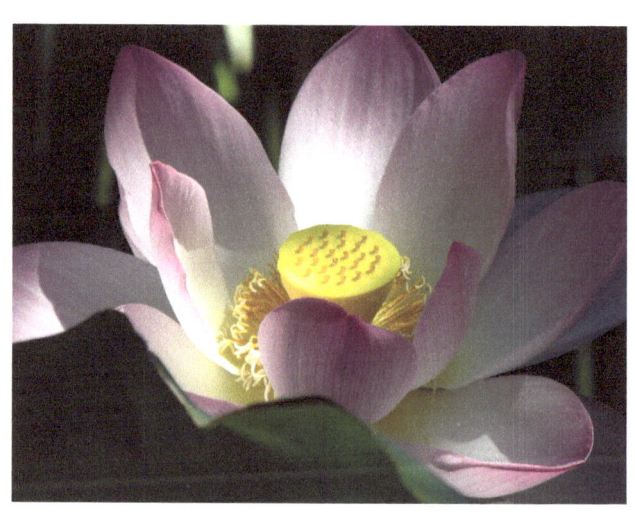

-THE END-

ABOUT THE AUTHOR

As a creative writer (both traditional and innovative), Deborah Johnson is a proven senior professional with integrity and a high work ethic. She has provided and will continue to provide a fresh perspective with a sound foundation in all her endeavors. A researcher, writer and speaker, Ms. Johnson has a love of the written word. She writes poetry and prose and enjoys writing opinion pieces on issues of the day.